STARTING AN ONLINE BUSINESS

From Idea to Profit: A Comprehensive Guide to Launching and Succeeding in the Digital Marketplace"

JONAS CHARLES KPABITEY

Copyright © 2024 JONAS CHARLES KPABITEY

No part of this publication may be reproduced, distributed, or transmitted in any form or by any means, including photocopying, recording, or other electronic or mechanical methods, without the prior written permission of the copyright owner, except in the case of brief quotations embodied in critical reviews and certain other noncommercial uses permitted by copyright law. For permission requests, please contact]
Phone number +233 (0) 555848312
+233 (0) 506692718
Email address:
CharlesWashington783@gmail.com

"In the vast landscape of opportunity, the digital realm offers a canvas for entrepreneurship unlike any before. Within these pixels lie the blueprints for dreams to flourish and fortunes to be forged.

CONTENTS

Title Page
Copyright
Epigraph
Introduction
Preface
Chapter 1   1
Chapter 2   4
Chapter 3   8
Chapter 4   13
Chapter 5   17
Chapter 6   20
Conclusion: 25
Epilogue   27
Afterword   29
About The Author   31

INTRODUCTION

In an increasingly interconnected world, the internet has emerged as a potent change agent, transforming how we live, work, and conduct business. The rise of internet entrepreneurship has created a new universe of opportunities, allowing people like you to start and grow successful digital firms. If you're reading this book, you're probably interested in beginning your own online business and realizing its enormous potential.

"Starting an Online Business" is a thorough guide to navigating the fascinating and ever-changing world of online entrepreneurship. Whether you're an aspiring entrepreneur seeking financial independence, a creative soul looking to share your passion with a global audience, or an established business owner ready to embrace the digital landscape, this book will equip you with the knowledge, tools, and strategies you need to embark on this transformative journey. Starting an online business has many advantages. It enables you to contact a large consumer base, cross geographical borders, and work with flexibility and freedom. The hurdles to entry are lower than ever before, and with the appropriate mindset and a good strategy, you can make your entrepreneurial aspirations a reality.

To start, we will assist you in defining your idea for an internet business, walk you through the process of choosing your specialty, and help you carry out market research. Subsequently, we will commence drafting a robust business plan that delineates practical measures to convert your concept into a feasible and enduring enterprise. We'll look at how to create a strong online presence through branding, digital marketing, and website building because a great online business starts with a solid foundation. Essentials of e-commerce will be covered, such as handling payments, merchandise, and shipping to guarantee smooth transactions and happy customers.

As we progress, we'll address the importance of setting up systems and processes that allow for scalability and growth. We'll discuss strategies for expanding your customer base, leveraging data analytics, and building a network of loyal customers.

Throughout this book, you'll find practical tips, real-life examples, and insightful case studies that bring the concepts to life. You'll gain insights into the mindset of a successful online entrepreneur and learn valuable lessons from those who have already walked the path to success.

Establishing an online business is a thrilling and fulfilling undertaking, but it also calls for commitment, tenacity, and an openness to change. Keeping up with the always-changing and dynamic digital scene is crucial. Are you prepared to start this life-changing adventure? This book is your road map to a successful internet business, regardless of your level of experience as an entrepreneur. Now let's get started, investigate the options, and learn how to make your ambitions for an internet business a reality. The adventure of your digital entrepreneurship begins now.

PREFACE

Starting an Online Business: From Idea to Profit. In today's digital world, the possibilities for starting and expanding a successful Internet business are endless. Whether you're a new entrepreneur or an aspiring business owner wishing to go from the traditional brick-and-mortar world to the online world, this book is your thorough guide to making your ideas a reality.

The internet has transformed how we interact, communicate, and conduct business. It has leveled the playing field, giving people like you the tools and platforms they need to reach a worldwide audience, make important relationships, and build thriving businesses from the comfort of their own homes. This book is intended to be a reliable companion as you embark on your internet business adventure. It will provide you with the information, insights, and practical solutions required to navigate the ever-changing digital landscape. Whether you're interested in e-commerce, digital services, affiliate marketing, or another type of online business, the ideas outlined on these pages are universally applicable.

Starting an internet business can be intimidating, especially if you're not familiar with the complexities of the digital world. However, with the correct mindset, advice, and a step-by-step strategy, you can successfully traverse the challenges and capitalize on the numerous opportunities that await. Throughout this book, we will look at the essential aspects of starting and growing an online business. Each chapter will cover vital topics like as ideation and market research, as well as website building, branding, marketing, and more, providing practical suggestions, real-world examples, and actionable methods.

Remember that starting a successful online business needs commitment, perseverance, and adaptability. It's a voyage that will put your entrepreneurial spirit to the test and take you outside of your comfort zone. With the correct mindset, a sound plan, and a willingness to learn and adapt, you can convert your internet company dreams into a rewarding and profitable reality. I encourage you to approach this transforming journey with an open mind and a sense of joy. Whether you want financial freedom, flexible work conditions, or the potential to make a significant difference in the lives of others, the world of online business has limitless opportunities.

So, let us plunge in together and open the doors to your internet company's success. Prepare to unleash your creativity, embrace innovation, and establish a thriving digital enterprise. Your path to Internet business success begins today

CHAPTER 1

The Online Business Landscape: Understanding Opportunities and Trends

The business world has seen a major transformation thanks to the internet, which has brought both new opportunities and problems for existing organizations and individuals. This chapter will examine the constantly changing world of Internet business, looking at important trends, new opportunities, and successful techniques.

E-commerce's Ascent The explosive growth of e-commerce has been one of the biggest trends in the Internet business sector. Traditional retail models have been challenged by the ease, global reach, and data-driven insights of e-commerce, enabling firms of all kinds to access clients globally. Global e-commerce sales are expected to increase from $3.3 trillion in 2019 to over $6.3 trillion by 2024, according to current industry forecasts. Growing consumer preferences, the proliferation of user-friendly e-commerce platforms, and the growing usage of mobile devices have all contributed to this explosive rise. Online shopping is becoming more and more popular due to its convenience, variety, and affordable prices.

The expansion of digital marketplaces In addition to direct-to-consumer e-commerce, digital marketplaces have evolved as a significant channel for online enterprises. Platforms like Amazon, eBay, and Etsy have given entrepreneurs and small enterprises access to large client bases, efficient logistics, and powerful selling tools. Online retailers can access new markets, decrease overhead expenses, and profit from the platform's built-in trust and reputation by using its reach and infrastructure. As customer confidence in digital marketplaces grows, this channel will expand further, providing an excellent opportunity for businesses to increase and diversify their sales.

The Rise of the Gig Economy

The online business landscape has also given rise to the gig economy, which allows freelancers, independent contractors, and small service providers to connect with customers and clients all over the world. Platforms such as Fiverr, Upwork, and Freelancer.com have created a flexible, on-demand workforce, allowing organizations to acquire specialized skills and experience as needed. This change to a more flexible, project-based workforce has resulted in numerous benefits, including cost savings, enhanced efficiency, and the ability to rapidly grow operations. However, it has prompted concerns about worker safeguards, benefits, and the long-term viability of this paradigm.

The Significance of Online Advertising The significance of digital marketing has grown for companies looking to draw in and keep consumers as the internet environment has changed. To increase brand awareness, drive traffic, and convert leads, tactics including influencer collaborations, social media marketing, content marketing, and search engine optimization (SEO) have become crucial. Companies are frequently in a better position to stand out in an increasingly congested online marketplace when they invest in a comprehensive digital marketing strategy that is catered to their target demographic and industry. Businesses may maximize their marketing efforts and achieve sustainable success by utilizing data-driven insights and continuously adjusting to the shifting digital world.

New Developments and Prospects

The world of online business is always changing, offering existing businesses and entrepreneurs new opportunities as well as problems. Here are a few new developments and prospective growth areas:

1. Personalisation and Customisation: Businesses that can successfully use data and AI to offer customized goods, services, and marketing messages are likely to gain a competitive edge. Consumers want more and more personalized experiences.

2. Sustainability and Social Responsibility: These are two topics that consumers, particularly younger ones, are paying more attention to. Companies that successfully incorporate these principles into their operations and branding will be in a position to draw in and hold on to customers who care about the environment and society.

3. Immersive Technologies: As augmented reality, virtual reality, and mixed reality (AR, VR, and MR) gain traction, businesses have new ways to offer immersive, interesting experiences that improve virtual try-ons, customer interactions, and product discovery.

4. The Internet of Things (IoT)Based on the increasing quantity of linked devices, companies can use IoT technology to enhance consumer experiences, streamline operations, and create novel product offerings.

5. Omnichannel Strategies: To offer a seamless and unified consumer experience, thriving companies are implementing omnichannel strategies, which involve seamlessly merging their online and offline presences.

CHAPTER 2

Defining Your Online Business Idea: Finding Your Niche

Any successful internet business starts with a well-defined concept and a thorough grasp of its target audience. To stand out and get your audience's attention in the crowded and competitive digital space, you must identify your specialty. You will find guidance in this chapter on how to define your idea for an internet business and identify a lucrative niche.

Finding Your Interest and Area of Specialisation Assessing your ideas is the first step towards identifying your online business. About what do you truly have a strong passion? What are your experiences, talents, or knowledge bases that you think others might find useful? A more sustainable and rewarding company venture can be achieved by matching your business idea with your areas of competence and passion. Take into account your interests, work experience, and personal problem-solving experiences. These may be excellent places to start when looking for a market niche in which you can provide original ideas, remedies, or goods.

Conducting Market Research

Market research should be started as soon as you have a broad notion of your possible business focus. Recognize unmet demands, evaluate the competitive environment, and determine whether your proposal is viable. Look for companies, goods, and services that are currently offering offerings in your niche online. Examine their pricing, target market, and offers. You'll be better able to spot market gaps and chances to set your company apart with this assistance. Surveys, interviews, and online forums are effective ways to interact with your target audience. Discover more about their inclinations, purchasing patterns, and areas of discomfort. Developing successful marketing plans and refining your offerings of goods and services will be made much easier with this information.

Evaluating the Potential Profitability

While passion and expertise are essential, the ultimate success of your online business will depend on its profitability. Carefully analyze the market size, pricing, and potential revenue streams to ensure your niche is viable and can support a sustainable business.

Consider the following factors when evaluating the profitability of your online business idea:

1. Market Size: Evaluate the target market's total size and potential for expansion. In general, larger markets with rising demand are more alluring.

2. Pricing and Margin: Examine your competitors' profit margins and pricing policies. Assess the potential for your company to sustain good margins and offer competitive pricing.

3. Revenue Streams: Determine possible sources of income and project their earning potential, such as product sales, affiliate marketing, subscriptions, or advertising.

4. Scalability: Assess how scalable your business plan is. Is it feasible for others to simply copy and expand your idea to reach a larger audience?

Differentiating Your Offering

Making your service stand out from the competition and giving your target audience something special is crucial in a crowded online market. Consider your competitors' advantages, disadvantages, and USPs carefully. Use your knowledge, past encounters, and consumer insights to create a distinctive strategy or angle that makes your company stand out. This might include developing cutting-edge features or products, providing a more individualized service, or concentrating on a particular niche.

Validating Your Idea

Before fully committing to your online business idea, it's crucial to validate its viability through real-world testing. This can involve:

1. MVPs and prototyping: Create a basic version of your product or service and get input from prospective clients.

2. Soft Launches: Slowly present your product to a narrow group of people while keeping an eye on their responses and involvement.

3. Crowdfunding Campaigns: Starting a crowdfunding campaign is a good way to find early investors and determine how interested the market is.

Your idea will be improved, any possible problems will be resolved, and you can make sure that your niche is appealing to your target market and profitable.

There are several common revenue streams that online businesses can leverage to generate income. Here are some of the most common ones:

1. Product Sales: Selling physical or digital products directly to customers is a fundamental revenue stream for many online businesses. This can include e-commerce stores, digital downloads (e-books, software, media), or subscription-based digital products.

2. Services: Offering professional services, consulting, or expertise-based offerings is a popular revenue stream for online businesses. This could include things like web design, digital marketing, coaching, or freelance services.

3. Advertising and Sponsorships: Monetizing website or platform traffic by selling advertising space or sponsorship opportunities to other businesses can be a reliable revenue stream, especially for content-focused online businesses.

4. Affiliate Marketing: Earning commissions by promoting and referring other companies' products or services to your audience is a common revenue stream for many online businesses, especially bloggers and influencers.

5. Subscriptions: Providing ongoing access to exclusive content, software, or membership benefits through a recurring subscription model can generate stable, predictable revenue for online businesses.

6. Licensing and Intellectual Property: Licensing your proprietary technology, content, or intellectual property to other businesses can be a lucrative revenue stream for online companies with valuable assets.

7. Events and Webinars: Hosting virtual or in-person events, workshops, or webinars can be an effective way for online businesses to generate revenue, especially when paired with additional product or service offerings.

8. Crowdfunding and Crowdsourcing: Platforms like Kickstarter and Indiegogo allow online businesses to raise funds from a community of supporters in exchange for exclusive products, experiences, or equity.

9. Data and Analytics: For online businesses with substantial audience data and insights, monetizing this information through data-driven products or services can be a valuable revenue stream.

The most successful online businesses often leverage a combination of these revenue streams, diversifying their income sources and reducing reliance on a single model. Careful analysis of your target market, competitive landscape, and unique business strengths can help you identify the most viable revenue streams for your online venture.

CHAPTER 3

Crafting your online business strategy: planning for success.

Developing a potent and well-thought-out online company plan is critical for navigating the changing and competitive digital landscape. A detailed strategy gives a clear path, allows you to spend resources more effectively, and boosts your prospects of long-term success. In this chapter, we will look at the important components of developing an internet company strategy that will put your venture up for long-term growth and success.

Define Your Vision and Mission

The cornerstone of your online business strategy is built on a clear vision and mission statement. Your vision statement should provide a compelling image of your long-term goals, explaining what you expect to accomplish. Your mission statement, on the other hand, should succinctly express your purpose and the distinct value you want to provide to your clients. By connecting your daily operations, decision-making, and strategic efforts with your vision and purpose, you can keep your online business focused, motivated, and true to its essential values.

Conduct a Comprehensive Market Analysis

The market study is critical for understanding the competitive landscape, recognizing opportunities, and building an informed online company plan. Gather detailed information on your target audience, competitors, industry trends, and emerging technologies that may have an impact on your organization. To acquire a full insight into your market, use a variety of research approaches, including consumer surveys, industry publications, and competitor analysis. This data will help you create your products or services, as well as your pricing and marketing tactics.

Establish Your Unique Value Proposition

In a congested online marketplace, your unique value proposition (UVP) is what distinguishes your company and convinces buyers to choose your offerings over competitors. Distil the unique benefits, services, or experiences you offer that address your target audience's specific demands and problem concerns. Creating a compelling UVP requires deep customer insights, a complete grasp of your competition, and a clear articulation of the value you provide. Make sure your unique selling proposition is prominently presented across all of your web platforms and integrated into your branding, marketing, and sales tactics.

Develop Your Online Business Model

Your online business model describes how you will make revenue, add value to your clients, and maintain a competitive advantage. Consider the numerous revenue streams, pricing structures, and operational processes that will allow your company to thrive in the digital environment. To select the best and most effective business strategy for your venture, consider e-commerce, subscription-based services, digital product sales, advertising, and affiliate marketing. Review and adapt your company model regularly in response to changing market conditions and customer preferences.

Outline Your Marketing and Sales Strategies

Effective marketing and sales tactics are essential for promoting customer acquisition, engagement, and loyalty in the online world. Create a thorough plan that incorporates a variety of digital marketing channels, including search engine optimization (SEO), social media, content marketing, email marketing, and paid advertising. Ensure that your marketing and sales efforts are in sync with your brand identity, unique value proposition, and target audience. To maximize your return on investment (ROI), constantly assess the efficacy of your campaigns, collect customer feedback, and fine-tune your plans.

Establish Your Operational Framework

Your internet business's success is also determined by the robustness of its operational foundation. This includes things like website and IT infrastructure, order fulfillment, customer service, and data management. Create and build efficient, scalable, and secure procedures that support your daily operations. Use technologies, software, and automation to optimize workflows, increase productivity, and deliver a consistent customer experience. Regularly assess and adjust your operating framework to stay up with technological improvements and changing client expectations.

Set Measurable Goals and Key Performance Indicators (KPIs)

Establish clear, quantifiable goals and key performance indicators (KPIs) to monitor your online business strategy's growth and success. These metrics should be in line with your vision, mission, and overall business goals, and they should be tracked and analyzed regularly. Website traffic, conversion rates, customer acquisition cost, average order value, customer lifetime value, and revenue growth are some of the most popular KPIs for online businesses. By routinely tracking and analyzing these metrics, you can make data-driven decisions, discover areas for improvement, and modify your plan as needed.

Continuously Adapt and Iterate

The Internet business scene is always changing, with new trends, technology, and consumer preferences emerging at a rapid pace. To ensure your venture's long-term success, your internet business approach must be fluid and adaptable. Review your plan regularly, collect client feedback, and keep track of industry changes. Be willing to make changes and iterate on your strategy to stay ahead of the competition and suit your target audience's changing wants.

Crafting a comprehensive and adaptable online business strategy is critical for navigating the changing digital landscape and setting your venture for long-term success. You may create the framework for a strong online business by defining your vision and goal, conducting rigorous market research, developing a unique value proposition, and designing a solid operational and marketing strategy. Remember to track your progress, adjust to changing conditions, and stay committed to providing outstanding value to your clients.

Here are some examples of successful online businesses that have adapted their strategies to changing market conditions:

1. Amazon: As one of the pioneering e-commerce giants, Amazon has consistently adapted its strategy to respond to evolving consumer preferences and emerging market trends. Initially focused on book sales, Amazon has expanded its offerings to include a vast array of product categories, digital services (e.g., Amazon Web Services, Prime Video), and even brick-and-mortar retail with the acquisition of Whole Foods. Amazon's ability to pivot and diversify its business model has been a key driver of its sustained success.

2. Netflix: From its origins as a DVD-by-mail rental service, Netflix has transformed itself into a leading global streaming platform. As consumer viewing habits shifted towards on-demand, digital content, Netflix quickly adapted its strategy, investing heavily in original content production and international expansion to stay ahead of the competition from traditional media companies and emerging streaming services.

3. Shopify: Shopify, the e-commerce platform provider, has demonstrated its adaptability by continuously enhancing its offerings to support the evolving needs of online merchants. As the COVID-19 pandemic drove a surge in online shopping, Shopify rapidly rolled out new features and tools to help its clients establish and grow their digital presence, such as expanded payment options, improved inventory management, and streamlined fulfillment capabilities.

4. Airbnb: The vacation rental platform Airbnb faced significant challenges during the COVID-19 pandemic, as travel restrictions and lockdowns severely impacted its core business model. In response, Airbnb quickly pivoted its strategy, focusing on domestic and local travel experiences, introducing flexible cancellation policies, and diversifying its offerings to include longer-term stays and remote work accommodations. These strategic adaptations enabled Airbnb to weather the crisis and emerge as a stronger, more resilient platform.

5. Peloton: Peloton, the connected fitness company, experienced exponential growth during the COVID-19 pandemic as consumers sought convenient, at-home workout solutions. However, as pandemic-related restrictions eased and consumer behavior shifted, Peloton had to adapt its strategy to address declining demand and inventory challenges. This included price reductions, cost-cutting measures, and the introduction of new, more affordable product offerings to maintain its competitive edge.

CHAPTER 4

Building Your Online Presence: Websites, Branding, and Marketing

In the digital age, having a strong online presence is critical for the success of every organization, regardless of its size or industry. Your online presence is the foundation for engaging with your target audience, exhibiting your brand, and driving business success. In this chapter, we'll look at the fundamentals of creating a good online presence, including website construction, branding, and marketing tactics.

Crafting an Impactful Website

Your website is frequently the initial point of interaction between your business and potential clients. It is critical to create a website that is visually appealing, user-friendly, and performance and discoverability-optimized.

When creating your website, remember the following excellent practices:

1. **Responsive Design:** Make sure your website is optimized for a consistent user experience on desktop, tablet, and mobile devices.

2. **Intuitive Navigation:** Organise your content logically and intuitively to help visitors discover the information they need.

3. **Engaging Content:** Create high-quality, educational, and visually appealing content that speaks to your target audience.

4. **Search Engine Optimisation (SEO):** Use efficient SEO tactics to increase your website's visibility and rating in search results.

5. **Conversion-Focused Design:** Include clear calls-to-action and

lead capture forms to encourage visitors to interact with your company.

6. Secure and Reliable: Prioritise website security, stability, and load times to ensure a dependable and delightful customer experience.

Establishing a Consistent Brand Identity

Your brand identity is the basis on which your internet presence is formed. It includes the visual and emotional elements that set your company apart and leave an indelible impact on your customers.

Important elements of a successful brand identity include:

1. Logo and Visual Assets: Create a distinct, distinctive logo as well as other visual components including color palettes, typography, and photography that reflect your brand's personality and values.

2. Messaging and Tone: Develop a consistent brand voice, tone, and messaging that appeals to your target audience and corresponds with your business goals.

3. Brand rules: Create a thorough set of brand rules that maintain uniformity across all touchpoints, including your website and social media, marketing materials, and customer interactions.

4. Coherent Brand Experience: Integrate your visual identity, messaging, and tone throughout all online and offline platforms to create a smooth and coherent brand experience.

Implementing Effective Digital Marketing Strategies

To increase visibility, engagement, and conversions, a comprehensive digital marketing plan must be developed and implemented.

Utilize a combination of the following channels and tactics.

1. Search Engine Optimisation (SEO): Improve your website's exposure and rating in search engine results by optimizing its content, technological elements, and structure.

2. Content Marketing: Create and share valuable, informative, and entertaining material to attract, educate, and nurture your target audience.

3. Social Media Marketing: Create a strong presence on relevant social media platforms and use them to increase brand awareness, promote community, and drive conversions.

4. Email Marketing: Create a targeted email marketing strategy to engage your audience, share updates, and nurture leads.

5. Paid Advertising: Supplement your organic efforts with targeted paid advertising campaigns across search engines, social media, and other digital platforms.

6. Influencer Partnerships: Work with relevant influencers, industry experts, or complementary companies to reach new audiences and build trust.

Fostering Customer Engagement and Loyalty

Creating a great online presence entails not just recruiting new clients, but also sustaining relationships and fostering customer loyalty. Implement techniques that foster long-term involvement and provide your clients with a great, memorable experience.

Tactics to foster customer engagement and loyalty include:

1. **Responsive Customer Service**: To create trust and loyalty, provide quick, personalized, and sympathetic customer help through all of your online channels.
2. **Engaging Community Interactions:** Create a feeling of community by actively engaging with your consumers, reacting to comments, and facilitating debate.
3. **Loyalty Programmes and Rewards**: Create loyalty programs and reward systems to drive repeat business and customer advocacy.

4. User-Generated Content: Promote and highlight user-generated content, such as reviews, testimonials, and social media posts, to increase social proof and boost your brand's legitimacy.

Continuous Optimisation and Adaptation.

The online scene is continuously changing, and your strategy for creating and sustaining an online presence must be as dynamic. Review the success of your website, branding, and marketing efforts regularly and make data-driven changes to keep your online presence relevant, effective, and consistent with your business objectives. Stay current on market trends, customer behaviors, and technical breakthroughs to discover areas for improvement and innovation. By constantly optimizing and adjusting your online presence, you can stay ahead of the competition and provide a consistently great experience for your customers.

CHAPTER 5

E-Commerce Essentials: Managing Products, Payments, and Logistics

As the digital world evolves, e-commerce has become an integral component of modern corporate strategies. Successful e-commerce endeavors necessitate a thorough understanding of the essential components that power their operations, such as product management, payment processing, and logistics. In this chapter, we'll look at the e-commerce basics that every online firm needs to know to succeed in today's competitive digital economy.

Effective Product Management

Products are the core of any e-commerce firm. Effective product management requires a multidimensional strategy to ensure that your products are well-curated, accurately displayed, and optimized for consumer interaction and sale.

1. Product Catalogue Organisation: Make your product catalog clear, intuitive, and searchable, so customers can easily navigate and locate what they're looking for.

2. Product Descriptions and Media: Create engaging product descriptions that showcase your offerings' essential features, benefits, and unique selling aspects. Complement these explanations with high-quality, visually attractive product photos and videos.

3. Product Inventory Management: Implement strong inventory management systems to keep stock levels accurate, track sell-through rates, and ensure client orders are fulfilled on schedule.

4. Product Pricing and Bundling: Price your products strategically to preserve competitiveness and sustainable profit margins. Consider giving product bundles or customization options to enhance the average order value.

5. Product Review and Ratings: Encourage and highlight customer evaluations and ratings to foster trust, social proof, and a better knowledge of consumer preferences.

Streamlined payment processing.

Seamless and secure payment processing is critical for creating trust in your clients and facilitating a pleasant checkout experience. Carefully select and implement the appropriate payment gateway and merchant services to support your e-commerce activities.

1. Payment Gateway Integration: Integrate a trustworthy payment gateway that accepts a variety of payment methods, including credit and debit cards, digital wallets, and alternative payment choices.

2. Secure Checkout Experience: Make sure your checkout process is optimized for user experience and security, including clear calls-to-action, straightforward navigation, and strong encryption methods.

3. Fraud Prevention and Chargeback Management: Implement fraud detection and prevention techniques to reduce the risk of fraudulent transactions while successfully managing any chargebacks that may arise.

4. Foreign Payment Support: If you have a global consumer base, consider integrating payment methods and currencies that are appropriate for your foreign audience.

5. Adaptable Pricing and Subscription Options: Provide adaptable pricing structures, such as recurring subscriptions, installment plans, or tiered pricing, to support a wide range of client preferences and purchasing behaviors.

Efficient logistics and fulfillment

Delivering products to clients on time and consistently is critical to e-commerce success. Create a strong logistics and fulfillment strategy to match consumer expectations and maintain the seamless functioning of your online business.

1. Inventory Storage and Warehousing: Form strategic alliances with fulfillment centers or third-party logistics providers to improve your product storage and distribution efficiency.

2. Order Processing and Shipping: Use efficient order processing systems and work with reputable shipping carriers to ensure accurate and fast order fulfillment.

3. Reverse Logistics and Returns Management: Establish a clear and customer-friendly returns policy, as well as simplified processes for processing product returns and exchanges.

4. Shipping Options and Costs: Provide several shipping options, including normal, expedited, and international delivery, at transparent and competitive costs.

5. Tracking and Delivery Updates: Give customers real-time order tracking and delivery updates to improve the post-purchase experience and increase trust in your e-commerce operations.

Continuous optimization and adaptation.

The e-commerce scene is always changing, and successful online firms must be flexible in altering their tactics to meet changing client preferences, technology improvements, and industry trends.

Review and optimize your product management, payment processing, and logistical operations regularly using customer feedback, sales data, and industry benchmarks.

Embrace developing technologies like artificial intelligence, automation, and predictive analytics to improve e-commerce operations and the overall customer experience.

CHAPTER 6

Scaling Your Online Business: Growth Strategies and Long-Term Success

As your online business acquires traction and builds a solid foundation, the next crucial stage is to focus on expanding and achieving long-term growth. Scaling your business entails deliberately extending your operations, client base, and revenue sources to seize opportunities and strengthen your market position.

Identifying Scalable Growth Opportunities

The first step in scaling your online business is determining which sectors have the most potential for scalable growth. Perform a thorough review of your current operations, customer data, and market trends to identify the most viable opportunities.

Some common scalable growth opportunities for online businesses include:

1. Product and Service Expansion: Use your current knowledge and customer insights to create new products or services that address changing client demands and preferences.

2. Geographic Expansion: Increase your reach by targeting new geographic areas, both domestic and foreign, to reach previously untapped client categories.

3. Diversification of Revenue Streams: To build a more strong and more resilient business model, consider adding new revenue streams such as subscriptions, e-commerce, digital advertising, or licensing.

4. Leveraging Strategic Partnerships: Work with complementary companies, influencers, or industry experts to gain access to additional distribution channels, resources, and consumer bases.

5. Adoption of Scalable Technologies: Invest in scalable technologies like automation, artificial intelligence, and cloud-based solutions to streamline processes and increase productivity.

Developing a Scalable Infrastructure

As your online business expands, it's critical to create a scalable infrastructure capable of handling greater demand, increased operational complexity, and rising client expectations.

This could involve the following major considerations:

1. Technology and IT Systems: Make sure your website, e-commerce platform, and backend systems can handle increasing traffic, transactions, and data management needs.

2. Operational Processes: Standardise your operational procedures, logistics, and customer service to ensure consistency and efficiency at scale.

3. Talent and Human Resources: Create a talent acquisition and management strategy to attract, retain, and empower the best workforce to support your growth ambitions.

4. Financial Management: Set up effective financial planning, budgeting, and reporting processes to control cash flow, maximize profitability, and secure growth finance.

5. Data-Driven Decision-Making: Use data analytics and business intelligence to make informed, data-driven decisions that guide your scaling efforts and track the effectiveness of your strategy.

Expanding Your Customer Base

Acquiring new clients and retaining old ones is critical for long-term growth. Implement customized marketing and customer acquisition techniques to reach a larger audience and maintain ongoing interactions with your customers.

Effective strategies for expanding your customer base include:

1. Content Marketing and Lead Generation: Create a content marketing plan that attracts, educates, and nurtures new customers across many digital channels.

2. Referral and Affiliate Programmes: Create well-designed referral and affiliate programs to encourage your existing customers and partners to refer new business.

3. Omnichannel Customer Engagement: Offer a consistent, personalized customer experience across all touchpoints, including your website, social media, email, and customer support.

4. Loyalty and Retention Initiatives: Use customer loyalty programs, personalized communication, and value-added services to build long-term customer connections and reduce churn.

5. Internationalization and Localization: Customise your offerings, marketing, and customer support to meet the specific demands and preferences of clients in different geographic regions.

Optimizing for Sustainable Growth

Scaling your internet business necessitates a careful balance of quick growth while retaining operational efficiency, financial viability, and customer pleasure. Implement a comprehensive optimization approach to ensure that your growth trajectory remains sustainable in the long run.

Key elements of a sustainable growth optimization strategy include:

1. Continuous Process Improvement: Review and streamline your operational workflows, logistics, and customer service regularly to increase productivity and reduce costs.

2. Financial Discipline and Profitability: Keep a close eye on profitability, cash flow management, and financial planning to help with your scaling efforts.

3. Performance Monitoring and Adjustment: Set key performance indicators (KPIs) and regularly assess the impact of your growth initiatives, making modifications as necessary.

4. Talent Development and Organisational Scaling: Invest in your team's professional development and training to guarantee that they can effectively assist your scaling initiatives.

5. Adaptability and Risk Management: Maintain agility and responsiveness to market changes, new trends, and potential risks that may affect your growth trajectory.

Exploring Inorganic Growth Opportunities

In addition to organic development tactics, consider researching inorganic growth alternatives that can help you scale faster and gain access to new capabilities, resources, or customer segments.

Inorganic strategies for growth may include:

1. Mergers and Acquisitions: Make strategic acquisitions of complementary firms or assets to broaden your product offerings, client base, or geographic reach.

2. Strategic Partnerships and Joint Ventures: Work with industry leaders, influential brands, or new startups to tap into their expertise, distribution channels, or technology.

3. Venture Capital and Private Equity Investment: Seek outside capital from investors to fuel your scaling efforts, gain access to new resources, and accelerate your growth trajectory.

Maintaining a Long-Term Mindset

Successfully scaling your online business necessitates a long-term, strategic mentality. While short-term growth is important, it is critical to strike a balance between fast successes and a long-term, future-oriented strategy.

Adopt the following methods to keep a long-term perspective and secure the long-term success of your internet venture:

1. Continuous Innovation and Adaptation: Foster an innovative culture, continuously watch industry trends, and change your business model and strategy to stay ahead of the pack.

2. Organisational Resilience: Enhance your team's competencies, promote a strong corporate culture, and establish organizational resilience to weather market swings and unanticipated problems.

3. Brand Equity and Customer Loyalty: To sustain growth, invest in building your brand, providing excellent customer experiences, and cultivating long-term customer relationships.

4. Financial Stability and Diversification: To preserve your internet business's sustainability, maintain a strong financial position, diversify your revenue streams, and look for chances for strategic investments or acquisitions.

CONCLUSION:

The Road Ahead for Your Online Business

Bravo! To turn your entrepreneurial aspirations into a successful internet firm, you must have done the necessary initial steps if you have progressed this far. It is an exciting and difficult trip to launch an online business, but if you follow the tactics and best practices in this book, you will be well-positioned to position your enterprise for long-term success and successfully traverse the ever-changing digital landscape.

Keep in mind that there is still more work to be done as you proceed. Establishing and growing a profitable Internet business demands a steadfast dedication to ongoing innovation, adaptability, and learning. Because the internet is a dynamic environment, entrepreneurs who can adapt to change, take prudent risks, and remain on top of trends tend to be the most resilient. Pay special attention to new developments in consumer behavior, technology, and trends that may affect your target market and sector. Continue to collect and evaluate data to improve the customer experience, streamline operations, and inform decisions. Encourage a culture of innovation within your company to enable your staff to come up with innovative ideas and put them into action.

Above all, keep your primary mission and values front and center. Allow them to influence your team's creativity, direct your strategic decisions, and help create your brand's distinct personality. You will gain a devoted following and establish your place in the cutthroat internet market by remaining true to your mission and never letting up on your commitment to providing outstanding value to your clients. Even though there may be challenges along the way, your internet business can succeed and leave a lasting impression if you have the correct attitude, plans, and methods in place. Accept the difficulties, acknowledge your accomplishments, and never stop pushing the envelope of what is conceivable. You have the power to create the future of your internet business; the digital world is your canvas.

As you set out on this fascinating entrepreneurial path, we send you our best wishes. May your internet company flourish, inspire, and develop while making a lasting impression on the digital world.

EPILOGUE

"As you near the end of your trip, remember that every step you took toward your internet company demonstrated your bravery, perseverance, and steadfast conviction in your idea. Whether you're celebrating victories or facing obstacles, let this epilogue serve as a reminder that the road to success isn't always straight, but every curve and turn shapes you into the entrepreneur you were intended to be. Accept the lessons gained, treasure the relationships created, and may your entrepreneurial spirit continue to fly in the vast expanse of the digital frontier."

AFTERWORD

"In this afterword, as you wrap up your trip through the pages of 'Starting an Online Business,' remember that the conclusion of this book is just the beginning of your entrepreneurial adventure. As you enter the digital arena equipped with knowledge, dedication, and creativity, remember that success is a never-ending process of adaptation and progress. Embrace the ever-changing environment of internet commerce, be tough in the face of adversity, and, most importantly, never lose sight of the enthusiasm that fueled your entrepreneurial spark. Your internet company career is just beginning, with each chapter shaped by your unyielding passion and entrepreneurial energy."

ABOUT THE AUTHOR

Jonas Charles Kpabitey

Born in the bustling city of Accra, Ghana, Jonas Charles Kpabitey discovered his passion for storytelling at a young age. Raised in a family that valued education and literature, Jonas immersed himself in books from an early age, fostering a deep appreciation for the power of words.

Jonas's journey as a writer began during his formative years at the University of Ghana. Inspired by the rich cultural tapestry of his homeland and the diverse experiences of his peers, Jonas found his voice as a storyteller, weaving tales that reflected the complexities of life in Ghana and beyond.

During his time at university, Jonas distinguished himself not only as a diligent student but also as a prolific writer. His keen observations of human nature and his ability to capture the nuances of everyday life soon caught the attention of readers and fellow writers alike.

Jonas delves into themes of identity, belonging, and the search for meaning in a rapidly changing world. Drawing on his own experiences and those of his peers, he crafts a narrative that resonates with readers of all backgrounds, inviting them to explore the universal truths that bind us together as human beings.

Beyond his literary pursuits, Jonas remains deeply committed to using his platform as a writer. Whether through his fiction or his activism, he continues to inspire others to embrace their own stories and to strive for a more inclusive and compassionate world.

As Jonas Charles Kpabitey continues to hone his craft and share his unique perspective with the world, his voice promises to be a beacon of hope and inspiration for generations to come.

www.ingramcontent.com/pod-product-compliance
Lightning Source LLC
Chambersburg PA
CBHW050249230526
45470CB00005B/2175